Beyond Newton

The Beyond Series
By Dr. Chuck Missler

Koinonia House

Beyond Newton
Part of *The Beyond Series*
© Copyright 2016 Koinonia House Inc.
Published by Koinonia House
P.O. Box D
Coeur d'Alene, ID 83816-0347
www.khouse.org

ISBN: 978-1-57821-656-7

All Scripture quotations are from the King James Version
of the Holy Bible.

PRINTED IN THE UNITED STATES OF AMERICA

Table of Contents

Chapter 1

Challenges to Astronomy

A man may imagine things that are false, but he can only understand things that are true, for if the things be false, the apprehension of them is not understanding.

- Isaac Newton

Every first-year physics student learns about Newton's laws.

1) An object at rest stays at rest and an object in motion stays in motion until it's acted on by an outside force.
2) There is a relationship between acceleration, mass and force. An object will accelerate when force is applied according to the simple formula F=ma.
3) Every action has an equal and opposite reaction.

Since childhood, we've pictured Sir Isaac Newton sitting under an apple tree, when a piece of fruit falls and hits him on the head. This moment in his life supposedly spawned his curiosity about the nature of gravity. Newton is famous for his laws of motion and for offering the world a version of calculus. More than anything else, however, Newton is famous for his Law of Universal Gravitation. Whether there is any truth to the apple story, large or small, we do know that Newton produced the view of gravity that held for centuries until Einstein upset Newton through his theory on general relativity.

In this book we are going to explore some challenges to the current astronomical models of our universe, and we are going to realize that there is far more to reality than what Newton or even Einstein foresaw. If we have seen farther, "it is by standing on the shoulders of giants," as Newton once said, but the greatest giant to give us a boost is the Word of God itself.

This book is the fourth in a series:

In *Beyond Time and Space* we overviewed Einstein's theories of relativity and the strange nature of light and space-time and hyperspaces. We talked about the nonlinearities of the world.

In *Beyond Coincidence* we discussed the anthropic principle and the many remarkable "coincidences" in the laws of physics and nature of the universe that seem to be designed for man. We considered the characteristics of our own planet that make life on Earth not just possible, but comfortable as well. We also considered the deliberate design found in the Word of God. We've shown that the prophecies in the Bible demonstrate that its 66 books had to have had an origin from outside our time domain. The Bible is a message system from beginning to end, and it has one Author.

Beyond Perception was an exploration of the microcosm, the nature of matter and the sub-atomic world. We considered the possibility that the visible world is a hologram, and it appears that our universe is a digital simulation, a three-dimensional mask that covers a deeper reality.

In *Beyond Newton*, we will leave the world of the small and explore space. We will borrow small pieces of the previous three books, but we will expand on them to challenge the myths of astronomy. We will be shocked to realize that much of what we know about astronomy isn't necessarily so.

Epistemology 101

"I can't believe *that!*" said Alice.

"Can't you?" the Queen said in a pitying tone. "Try again: draw a long breath, and shut your eyes."

Alice laughed. "There's no use trying," she said: "one can't believe impossible things."

"I daresay you haven't had much practice," said the Queen. "When I was your age, I always did it for half-an-hour a day. Why, sometimes I've believed as many as six impossible things before breakfast."

In his famous 1871 book, *Through the Looking Glass*, author Lewis Carroll continues the craziness he began in *Alice's Adventures in Wonderland* (1865). On the other side of the mirror, in the world of chess pieces, Alice becomes the imaginary being. She meets Tweedledum and Tweedledee, finds the Jabberwocky poem full of strange words, and meets Humpty Dumpty, unicorns and other fantastic creatures. All Alice *thought* she knew is upended in this strange world on the other side of her reflection.

What do we actually know about our own reality?

Epistemology is the fancy word for the study of knowledge – its origin, its scope, and its limits. The problem with our fallible human knowledge is that it tends to change over time. During the ages, different cultures have "known" that the earth was flat, that the Sun and other planets revolved around the Earth, and that Newton had an apple hit him in the head.

In the 17th century A.D., it was believed that all combustible substances contained a particular material that was released when they were burned. In the early 1700s, one Georg Ernst Stahl called this burnable material "phlogiston" and he promoted the idea that wood was made of wood ash and phlogiston, while rustable metals were made of metallic ash and phlogiston.

Whether phlogiston was an actual physical thing or just a principle, the air involved was considered merely responsible for carrying off the phlogiston freed by the burning process.

Within a hundred years, however, phlogiston was cast aside as an explanation for why things burned. In the late 18th century, Antoine Lavoisier carefully measured the weights of various substances that went through oxidation or reduction reactions, and he demonstrated that oxygen was the culprit involved.

Wrong ideas often last longer than they should because we humans tend to get hooked on ideas rather than on truth. People in history who believed that the Earth was flat should have read the Bible:

> *It is he that sitteth upon the circle of the earth,*
> *and the inhabitants thereof are as grasshoppers;*
> *that stretcheth out the heavens as a curtain,*
> *and spreadeth them out as a tent to dwell in:*
>
> Isaiah 40:22

Wrong Ideas – Geocentrism

For millennia people believed that the Earth was the center of the solar system. Ptolemy of Alexandria developed the geocentric model in his works *Almagest* and *Planetary Hypotheses*. His picture of the solar system was known ever after as the Ptolemaic Model. For the next 1400-

1500 years, people believed as a matter of course that the Sun (and the rest of the sky) revolved around Earth every day. The Sun rose in the morning on one side of the planet and set on the other side in the evening. It took quiet Copernicus and loud Galileo to point out facts that required the alternative: Earth and other planets revolved around the Sun.

Yet, acceptance of the Copernican cosmology took quite a long time despite the fact that it fit careful observation of the facts much better than the model Ptolemy had offered. Copernicus first wrote about his heliocentric ideas in the early 1500s, and it was a full century later that Kepler supported those ideas with discussions on the elliptical orbit of Mars. About the same time, Galileo affirmed Copernicus through the use of a telescope. Even then, Copernicus' heliocentric theory was banned in 1616, and it took most of the 17th century for the idea that the Earth revolved around the Sun to take root in people's minds. Isaac Newton helped cement the idea with his work on gravitation, but it took until 1758 for the Roman Catholic Church to finally end its prohibition on books that taught heliocentrism.

Poor Ptolemy of Alexandria. He has gone down in history as the scientist who got it wrong on two fundamental truths in science. He was incorrect about the Earth as the center of the solar system, and he argued against the possibility of four dimensions.

Wrong Ideas – Aether

For many moons, astronomers and cosmologists believed the universe was filled with a material called the *aether*. Light was understood to be a wave, which meant it needed a medium through which it could travel, like waves on a cosmological pond. Aether was considered the pond through which light traveled across the universe. The aether was seen as an absolute reference frame in respect to the rest of the universe; everything had its speed in reference to the aether.

In 1887, the Michelson-Morley experiment attempted to measure the speed of aether itself. Michelson and Morley expected that as light traveled *with* the aether, it would race along faster, and as it traveled *against* the aether, it would move slower. They set up a detection device with a light source, mirrors and a telescope, and they found that no matter where the Earth was in its rotation around the Sun, the light always traveled at the same speed. This was an early experiment that demonstrated that light travels at the same speed in all inertial reference frames – and it all but disproved the existence of "aether."

Wrong Ideas – Infinite Speed of Light

The speed of light itself has been a matter of confusion and controversy. Philosophers and scientists including Kepler, Descartes and Galileo used reasoned arguments that the speed of light was instantaneous. In 1676, Danish astronomer Ole Rømer made observations about the orbit of Jupiter's moon Io, however, that led him to conclude the speed of light had a finite measurement. Io's whirling spin around Jupiter takes just 42 ½ hours per revolution, and the precise time Io disappears behind Jupiter can be measured. Rømer found that it took longer for the reflective light from Io to reach the Earth when Jupiter was far away from Earth than it took when Jupiter was near. This meant the light couldn't be arriving to the Earth instantaneously; it took a few minutes. Rømer sent his data to his friend Dutch astronomer and mathematician Christiaan Huygens, who calculated that light sped along at 16 2/3 Earth-diameters per second – about 132,000 miles per second. This value was off by about 1/3 of the correct value of 186,000 mps, because the exact distance of the planets wasn't known at that time, but Huygens got into the right ballpark.

In 1728 James Bradley noticed that the positions of stars seemed to change over the course of a year. He carefully watched a star in the constellation Draco, then other stars as well, and he used his knowledge of the Earth's speed around the Sun to calculate the speed of light as 301,000 km/s. In 1849, Armand Fizeau used mirrors and a spinning wheel setup to measure the speed of light at 315,000 km/s and Leon Foucault tried a similar experiment with rotating mirrors, narrowing the speed of light to 298,000 km/s.

Light is known as one of the fundamental constants of nature. Yet, we've learned in recent years that the constants of nature aren't so constant. The speed of light in a vacuum appears to have slowed down over the centuries, as documented by Barry Setterfield and Trevor Norman.[1] John Webb in Sydney has spent years determining that the fine structure constant "alpha" fluctuates depending on which direction researchers look into the heavens. In January of 2006, Webb and fellow physicist John D. Barrow published an article in *Scientific American* with the astonishing title: "Inconstant Constants."[2] Barrow and Webb make the case that physical "constants" like the speed of light can fluctuate after all. The article declares:

> ... *One implication is that the constants we observe may not, in fact, be the truly fundamental ones. Those live in the full higher-dimensional space, and we see only their three-dimensional shadows.*[3]

That's exciting. The observable physical universe is apparently just a mask that hides a deeper reality.

We need to be careful to follow the evidence. We should never jump to conclusions based on only a few facts, of course. We should investigate things thoroughly, and we should be open to embrace the reality of the situation, whatever it is.

The important take away from all of this – beyond the brief astronomy history lesson – is that it can take the world 50 years or more to embrace the truth behind the meaning of empirical data. People have a tendency to cling to their favorite belief systems long after experimental evidence requires the contrary. As humans, we have this tendency to throw out the information that doesn't fit with our pet theories. We shouldn't do that; we should listen to whatever is true.

Today, the prevailing scientific theory about our origins states that we evolved from amino acids in an ancient sea. This is probably not true. The evidence doesn't support biogenesis – the development of life from non-life. In fact, every observation we have made declares that new life only comes from existing life.

Michael Denton, Philip Johnson, Michael Behe and an ever-growing number of scientists and researchers have written on the problems with a theory of undirected evolution. It has become increasingly clear that the complex organization of biological life requires engineering. It's ridiculous to think that the life we see around us designed itself through natural processes, yet that's precisely what is still taught in our schools. Our whole society presumes it to be true, contrary to the observed facts. Physics students are still taught that the constants are constant, despite the growing collection of data that say otherwise. Human beings don't like change. It takes a long time for the myths of any culture to give way to reality.

Chapter 2

The Nebular Hypothesis

How did our solar system form? The popular answer to that question is a myth – one that should never have anchored itself in the public imagination. The Nebular Hypothesis goes something like this: "Some 4 billion years ago, the sun ejected a tail, a filament of material that cooled and collected into balls of matter that formed the planets." This is the typical explanation of the solar system still taught in universities today, but where did it come from?

Famous astronomer Immanuel Kant is credited with the Nebular Hypothesis, but he didn't invent it himself. In 1734, mining engineer Emanuel Swedenborg (1688-1772) published his *Prodromus Philosophiae Retiocinantis de Infinito et Cause Creationis* in Latin, in which he describes an alternate view of the creation of the universe. Swedenborg was a mystic in the negative sense. He claimed to be a Christian having visions, but he collected information about the supposed origin of the universe after having séances with spiritual beings that claimed to inhabit Jupiter and Saturn and other planets. His books *Arcana Coelestia* and *Earths in the Universe* describe some of the discussions with these other spiritual beings. Unfortunately, these "angels" gave Swedenborg a wide range of ideas that denied the straightforward interpretation of the Scriptures. Instead, they led him to regard the historical narratives of Moses as symbolic and filled with secret, hidden knowledge. Swedenborg came up with the idea that the planets formed from material that ejected out of the Sun, and the Sun itself was formed from a spinning nebula.

Swedenborg's claims of visions impressed the people around him. We know, however, that when Swedenborg was 23 years old, he had an opportunity to spend several weeks at the home of Edmund Halley, the astronomer after whom Halley's Comet is named. Swedenborg did have some astronomy background when he wrote his alternative ideas about how the planets originated.

Swedenborg had an influence on Kant, who alternately praised and demonized the mystic. Twenty years after Swedenborg's *Prodromus*, Kant published his *General History of Nature and Theory of the Heavens* (1755), in which he describes the Nebular Hypothesis. Kant sanctified the idea, and Pierre Laplace did the same, giving the faulty idea greater credibility than it would have had otherwise. These scientists were both capable of double checking the math, but they failed somewhere along the line. There are many problems with the Nebular Hypothesis, which neither of these great men exposed as they should have.

The Nebular Hypothesis gained widespread respectability despite the fact that it includes very serious mathematical errors. We've seen an increasing number of problems as we've learned more about the solar system, but subsequent writers have sought to explain away the difficulties rather than throwing the idea out altogether.

Nebular Troubles

Angular Momentum is Discordant

The angular momentum of an object can be calculated by its mass x velocity x distance from center of mass. Angular momentum is always conserved, which is why ice skaters spin faster when they pull their arms in; they've just shortened the distance to their center of mass, increasing their velocity. The Sun contains about 99.87% of the mass of our solar system. Nearly all of it. The Sun has a mass of 1.99×10^{30} kg, more than 745 times the combined mass of all the planets. Yet, the Sun contains less than 4% of the angular momentum of the solar system.

Planet	Mass (kg)	Orbital Ang. Moment. (kg m²/sec)	% of Solar System Orb Ang. Moment.
Mercury	3.30×10^{23}	9.1×10^{38}	0.003%
Venus	4.87×10^{24}	1.8×10^{40}	0.058%
Earth	5.97×10^{24}	2.7×10^{40}	0.087%
Mars	6.42×10^{23}	3.5×10^{39}	0.011%
Jupiter	1.90×10^{27}	1.9×10^{43}	61.2%
Saturn	5.68×10^{26}	7.8×10^{42}	25.1%
Uranus	8.68×10^{25}	1.7×10^{42}	5.48%
Neptune	1.02×10^{26}	2.5×10^{42}	8.05%
	Total: 2.67×10^{27}	Total: 3.1×10^{43}	

That's a strange thing. If enough nebular dust to form the Sun collapsed into a fiery ball, it should have spun faster as its diameter got smaller (as the ball grew denser). Yet, the angular momentum in our solar system is concentrated in the orbital angular momentum of the planets, while the Sun spins at a much slower rate.

Even worse, there is hardly any continuity between the rotations and revolutions of the various planets. The combined orbital momentum of all the planets is about 28 times larger than the Sun's angular momentum. Our own moon has an orbital angular momentum four times greater than Earth's rotational angular momentum, but Jupiter has the opposite phenomenon; its rotational momentum is nearly 154 times larger than the orbital angular momentum of its four largest moons. If the planets formed from the same spinning nebular material, there should be a relationship between the angular momentum of the planets and the Sun. There should be a relationship between the momentum of the moons and their host planets. In both cases, the expected mathematical harmony is simply not there.

Name	Mass (kg)	Rotational Ang. Moment. (kg m²/sec)	Orbital Ang. Momentum of Satellites (kg m²/sec)	Rotational/ Orbital momentum
Sun	1.99×10^{30}	1.1×10^{42}	(planets) 3.1×10^{43}	1/28
Earth	5.97×10^{24}	7.1×10^{33}	(moon) 2.9×10^{34}	1/4
Jupiter	1.90×10^{27}	6.9×10^{38}	(moons) 4.49×10^{36}	153 2/3

This is a real problem. We can measure it. What's more, this was known at the time of Laplace more than a century ago, but he didn't take time to think through the problems before embracing the Nebular Hypothesis.

Planet Sizes Don't Fit

It gets worse. James Jeans (1877-1946) pointed out that the outer planets are larger than the inner ones. Jupiter is almost 6,000 times as massive as Mercury. It's almost 3,000 times as massive as Mars. That's hard to explain, because we would expect the most massive planets to hang around near the Sun and the lightest ones to fly far away. Instead, mighty Jupiter sits immediately past tiny Mars. This is a difficulty for all current theories that suggest the planets came from the Sun.

Oxygen Levels Don't Match

In 2004, NASA's Genesis mission collected solar wind debris and found that oxygen levels were much higher in the Sun than elsewhere. ^{16}O is the most common oxygen isotope, but it is apparently far more dense in the Sun than in Earth or Mars or the moon.[4] Researcher Kevin McKeegan told *Space Daily*:

> *We found that Earth, the moon, as well as Martian and other meteorites which are samples of asteroids, have a lower concentration of the O-16 than does the sun... The implication is that we did not form out of the same solar nebula materials that created the sun – just how and why remains to be discovered.*[5]

Planet Spin-rates and Tilts are Diverse

If all the planets came from the same solar nebula, we'd expect them to all spin in the same direction at a reasonably similar rate – at least relative to their masses and sizes. Instead, there are three different sets of spinning rates among the planets of our solar system. Earth and Mars spin at nearly the same rate, with a day-length of about 24 hours. Jupiter and Saturn appear to be a pair with a day-length of about 10 hours. (Which, considering their great size, means they are both spinning at a very high velocity compared to Earth.) Neptune and Uranus also seem tuned to each other, making a single rotation every 16-17 hours. Mercury and Venus, on the other hand, are out on their own. Mercury makes a single rotation every 59 Earth days, and Venus revolves around the Sun faster than it makes a single turn on its axis.

Earth and Mars have a virtually identical axial tilt. Earth is angled at 23.5° and Mars at 25.2°. This tilt gives us our seasons of winter, spring, summer, and autumn. Saturn and Neptune are fairly close to Earth and Mars with tilts of about 27° and 28° respectively, while Jupiter and Mercury have hardly any tilt at all. Venus also stands straight up in reference to the Sun, except that it rotates clockwise while the rest of the planets rotate counter-clockwise. It is therefore said to have a 177° (nearly 180°) tilt. Uranus lies almost directly on its side, and its rotation is considered retrograde like Venus' because its tilt is greater than 90°. Particularly interesting is that Uranus' largest moons are also tilted at about 98°. Astronomers have a variety of suggestions to explain away these unexpected facts about the planets – but taken at face value, they contradict what would be predicted by the Nebular Hypothesis.

Planet	Rotation	Axial Tilt (degrees)	Density (g/cm³)
Mercury	58.79 days	0	5.427
Venus	243.69 days	177.36	5.243
Earth	23.93 hours	23.45	5.515
Mars	24.62 hours	25.19	3.933
Jupiter	9.93 hours	3.13	1.326
Saturn	10.66 hours	26.73	0.687
Uranus	17.24 hours	97.77	1.270
Neptune	16.11 hours	28.32	1.638

Chapter 3
The Red Planet

Mars is a particularly interesting planet. It seems closely paired up to Earth, with a similar rotation period and tilt, and a year-length that is almost twice that of Earth. Mars has maintained these similarities to Earth while showing signs of a heavy-handed history. A full 93% of its craters lie in one hemisphere while only 7% pockmark the other side. It would appear that more than 80% of Mars' craters occurred within a single half hour. What happened?

The planet Mars is a mystery. This fourth planet from the Sun has a high iron content, which has given it a distinctive red color. It terrified the earliest civilizations, and its influence on their minds is memorialized in its name: Mars, the Roman god of war. Mars was the Baal of the Old Testament, a menacing god to be feared.

Scientific historians tend to fall into a two categories: uniformitarians and catastrophists. Uniformitarians cling to the idea that natural processes create steady change over billions of years. That's one philosophy. Catastrophists, on the other hand, believe that the universe has been subjected to a series of catastrophic events. According to the Bible, the history of the Earth and the universe is one of catastrophe.

Ancient Catastrophes

There have been a series of catastrophes on the planet Earth. We find Peleg mentioned in the genealogy of Genesis 11. Peleg was born 101 years after the Flood, and during his lifetime, "the earth was divided." About 1877 B.C. Sodom and Gomorrah were destroyed by raining fire and brimstone. The Exodus plagues hit Egypt in 1447 B.C. and in about 1404 B.C., Joshua told the Sun and Moon to stand still, and they did. Both Amos and Zechariah tell us that an earthquake shook the land during the days of Uzziah, King of Judah.

The Israelites and their ancestors were not alone on the planet at this time. Many of these events would have had far-reaching impact, touching peoples around the world. When God moved the shadow back ten degrees for Hezekiah, that indicates some massive event taking place in the heavens.

We can look at the moon through a pair of binoculars and see that it's been beat up. As we send probes to the other planets, we see the same thing. They are scarred with craters. Our solar system is a rough neighborhood. Under a constant rain of interplanetary debris, Earth itself still collects about 100 tons of extraterrestrial material per day. More than 100 craters can be found on our ocean-clothed planet. A crater one mile across plummets into the ground near Winslow, Arizona, and another on the Yucatan Peninsula is an inconceivable six miles in diameter. The impact explosion was the equivalent of a 100-megaton bomb. A giant meteor hits the earth every 300 years or so, but two-thirds of these land in the ocean and leave no trace.

The ancients were sensitive to these falling rocks that blazed through the atmosphere and smashed into the ground. A meteorite landed in what is now the city of Mecca in Saudi Arabia. Two thousand years before Muhammad, the people created the Ka'aba in its honor. The Muslims adopted the shrine as their own, declaring that Abraham and Ishmael had built it, and today millions of Muslims still make their hajj to the Ka'aba to worship.

Cairo in Egypt is the site of the great pyramids. It's noteworthy that "Cairo" is the Egyptian equivalent of Mars. In Athens, we find the Areopagus. Paul speaks to the people there in Acts 17. Ares is the Greek equivalent of Mars, and that's why the location is called "Mars Hill."

We all know the story of Joshua, the successor to Moses. After Jericho, the Israelites fought a series of battles, and the remaining nations allied themselves under Adonizedek, king of Jerusalem.

Joshua 10 describes a climactic battle in the valley of Beth Horon, which I like to call the "Martial Arts" in the Battle of Beth Horon:

> *And the LORD discomfited them before Israel, and slew them with a great slaughter at Gibeon, and chased them along the way that goeth up to Bethhoron, and smote them to Azekah, and unto Makkedah. And it came to pass, as they fled from before Israel, and were in the going down to Bethhoron, that the LORD cast down great stones from heaven upon them unto Azekah, and they died: they were more which died with hailstones than they whom the children of Israel slew with the sword.*

Joshua 10:10-11

Interesting! Giant stones fell from heaven. What makes this a greater miracle isn't just that stones fell from heaven conveniently during the battle, but that the stones only hit the fleeing enemy of Israel. The verses that follow are even more astounding.

> *Then spake Joshua to the LORD in the day when the LORD delivered up the Amorites before the children of Israel, and he said in the sight of Israel, Sun, stand thou still upon Gibeon; and thou, Moon, in the valley of Ajalon. And the sun stood still, and the moon stayed, until the people had avenged themselves*

upon their enemies. Is not this written in the
book of Jasher? So the sun stood still in the
midst of heaven, and hasted not to go down
about a whole day.

Joshua 10:12-13

How many of us believe that? The more we know about astronomy and astrophysics and orbits, the more we recognize how truly tough this passage is. The Sun and Moon paused in the sky for what appeared to be an entire day. If the Earth's rotation slowed on its axis, unimaginable catastrophes would have followed – with worldwide effects. Yes, God holds all things together, and He can handle these difficulties, but this is a tough story to comprehend as a scientist. It turns out that the Earth's rotation did not have to slow. All that was required was to change Earth's precession a little in its elliptical orbit around the Sun, and this would have accomplished the same thing.

Earth and Mars

Earth and Mars have an interesting relationship. It is believed that early in history, Earth's orbit was 360 days and Mars' orbit was 720 days. They were in "resonance" with each other. Resonance orbits act just like tuning forks. If you tap a tuning fork and hold it in the air, it will cause another tuning fork with the same frequency to hum, even from across room. Orbits are the same way. They tend to become harmonic in their rotation.

Remember that the orbits are elliptical, and every now and then – every 108 years – Mars and Earth would have swung closely by one another. If they came close to each other in the spring, it would be during the spring equinox – about March 20th or 21st after perihelion. Each time this happened, Mars would lose a little energy and Earth would gain a little energy. However, sometimes they would pass each other in the fall, around October 25th, and this time Earth would lose a little energy and Mars would gain it back.

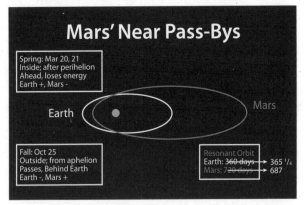

Theoretically this continued for millennia. By modeling the orbital resonance of these two planets, we find the pull of Mars and Earth on each other during near pass-by gives us an explanation for catastrophic events throughout ancient history. Something happened in 701 B.C., however, that added several more days to Earth's year and threw off this harmonic resonance.

Now, Earth has a year of 365 ¼ days and Mars has a year of 687 days. The orbits are no longer in perfect resonance, and the two planets no longer pass closely to each other as they did thousands of years ago, but the evidence for this ancient harmony can be seen in the calendars of past civilizations – as well as in their fear of the red planet.

Ancient Calendars

Ancient calendars offer us a variety of clues about astronomical changes in the past. We discovered that the calendars of many major civilizations were based on 360-day years, typically made up of 12 months with 30 days each. In 701 B.C., three centuries after King David, something happened to change the Earth's revolution around the Sun, and these ancient calendars made adjustments to deal with the sudden addition of five days to the year.

King Hezekiah ruled Israel from 715-686 B.C. Fifteen years before he died, however, in 701 B.C., Hezekiah came near to death. Isaiah the prophet came and prayed for him, and God gave him a sign; the shadow of the Sun would return backwards 10 degrees. Something huge happened in the heavens on that day – what exactly, we can't say. We simply know that from that day onward, the Earth's revolution around the Sun lengthened from 360 to 365 ¼ days, and the ancient calendars had to be modified to take the change into account.

Most of the calendars began in the spring with March, which the Romans named Martius after the planet Mars. Aprilia was dedicated to Venus, Maius was Mercury, and June was named for Jupiter's wife Juno. Mars long held the position of prominence as the first month of the year.

The medieval calendars in England continued to treat March as the first month until A.D. 1752. The Anglo-Saxons described March as the elective lengthened month (from which we get the term "Lent"). In Scotland, January replaced March as the first month in A.D. 1599, and Charles IX of France replaced March with January in 1564.

Even the days of the week give Mars first honor. Sunday was named for the Sun, Monday for the Moon, and Tuesday was named by the Teutonic tribes after *Tues*, the proto-Germanic name for Mars. Mercury / Odin is honored on Wednesday (Latin: *dies Mercurii*). The Teutonic version of Jupiter, Thor, is given *Thorsdag*, and *Freryrdag* is after a very old name for Venus. Finally, Saturday is Saturn's day. Even in the days of the week, Mars is given first cut after the Sun and Moon themselves, and is then followed by Mercury, Jupiter, Venus, and Saturn.   •

Every year, the planets fly across our skies without causing any trauma. What made those distant cultures so frightened of the planets, especially Mars the god of war, who is constantly given first rank?

Ancients and the Planets

Today we know that the planets are just balls of rock and gas, but the ancient peoples worshiped them. They were fascinated with the stars and planets. Astrology was a widespread part of religious observation, and all cultures appeared to be terrified of the planets, especially the planet Mars.

Why was Mars such a big deal? How many readers of this book can even point out Mars in the night sky without looking it up online first? It's easy to point out the Big Dipper. It's not so simple to discern between Venus and Jupiter without doing a little homework first, because the planets move through the sky and the positions of the planets are just not important to us in our daily lives. The movements of the planets were *not* incidental to the ancients, though. They feared them, particularly Mars, which is clearly demonstrated in the names of Mars/Aries' sons. The Greeks called them Phobos (terror) and Deimos (panic) – and the two small moons of the planet Mars are named after them.

It may have been that Mars once swept closer to the Earth than it does today, back when the two planets danced by each other in their resonating orbits, and there's an interesting bit of evidence of this in a familiar storybook.

The moons of Mars are tiny and invisible to the naked eye. Galileo missed them when he used the first series of telescopes in the early 1600s. He was able to see the four huge moons of Jupiter and the rings of Saturn – which are fairly large objects in the sky. It took Herschel's new and improved telescope to finally discover the planet Uranus in 1781 and two of its moons six years later. In 1846, Le Verrier discovered Neptune and one of its moons. It wasn't until 1877 that Asaph Hall was finally able to spy the two tiny, dark moons of Mars with a brand new telescope at the U.S. Naval Observatory.

This is why it's surprising that we find those two moons described in a satire by Jonathan Swift 150 years before they were seen by a modern telescope.

Jonathan Swift published a set of essays called *Gulliver's Travels* in 1726. We think of these as children's stories, but they were written as a collection of political satires making fun of 18th century England. We're most familiar with the Lilliputians, but in Gulliver's third voyage, he visits a place called Laputa. The inhabitants of Laputa are high-minded scientists. They are astronomers and they make fun of London, because they know about the two moons of Mars and the people in London don't.

It's just a story, except that it details the size and the revolutions of these two moons of Mars. While not precise, Swift's account is close enough to argue more than mere coincidence is involved.

Mars' moon Deimos is less than 8 miles in diameter and Phobos is not much larger – only about 14 miles across. Phobos is closer to Mars and Deimos is farther out. Phobos is the darkest object in the solar system and reflects about 3% of the light that hits it, but both moons have a very low albedo. Phobos is tiny – only 100th of the width of our Moon – and it flies around Mars once every 7.65 hours. What's more, it zooms around Mars backwards. It's the only moon in the solar system to rise in the west and set in the east, and it moves so fast that it flies around Mars several times in one 24.6-hour Martian day. Deimos, the outer Martian moon, revolves around Mars once every 30 hours and 18 minutes. Like our own moon, both Martian moons rotate so that the same side always faces Mars.

Asaph Hall did not discover the two moons of Mars until 1877, yet Jonathan Swift described them in *Gulliver's Travels* 151 years beforehand. In chapter three of the *Voyage To Laputa*, Swift says:

> *They have likewise discovered two lesser stars,*
> *or satellites, which revolve about Mars; whereof*
> *the innermost is distant from the center of the*
> *primary planet exactly three of his diameters,*

*and the outermost, five; the former revolves
in the space of ten hours, and the latter in
twenty-one and a half; so that the squares of
their periodical times are very near the same
proportion with the cubes of their distance from
the center of Mars; which evidently shows them
to be governed by the same law of gravitation
that influences the other heavenly bodies.*

Swift is referring to Kepler's Law of Motion
as it was understood in those days. Swift knew
Newton, Halley, and Winston personally, and
he could have made calculations about the
moons' periodical times based on what would
have been expected based on Kepler. At the same
time, Swift amazingly describes two moons –
not one or three or five. Swift's descriptions are
not precise; Phobos circles the planet in 7 hours
and 39 minutes, not 10 hours, but Swift's details
were certainly close enough to make one wonder.
Our own moon takes 29 days to circle our
planet. A lunar revolution of less than half a day
seems almost outrageous. What's more, Phobos
is drawing closer to Mars at a rate of 1.8m every
100 years, so its orbit was longer in the past.
Swift's descriptions seem much closer than we'd
expect of pure guesswork.

It's possible that Jonathan Swift had access
to myths and records that he assumed were just
legend, and he used them for his satire, throwing
in Kepler's laws for the fun of it. He probably

didn't realize that the legends he drew upon were actually eye witness accounts. The planet Mars would have had to be only 70-80,000 miles from the Earth, however, for any ancient peoples to see those moons with the naked eye. This follows the idea that Mars once passed very closely to the Earth, causing the ancient peoples to fear its terrifying approach.

On that long day of Joshua in Joshua 10, a third of a million men fought at Beth-Horon. In October 25th 1404 B.C., Mars was on a polar pass over Earth at 70,000 miles. That's very close. When Mars came near, it would have appeared to rise 50 times the size of the moon. It would have caused severe earthquakes and land tides, and a polar shift of about 5 degrees would have lengthened the day. Meteors followed at about 30,000 miles an hour – miraculously hitting only the enemies of Israel.

Chapter 4
A Byte of Epistemology

In modern physics under Einstein, we know we live in four dimensional space-time. Space-time can be curved in the presence of matter, and it follows a Riemannian geometry rather than Euclidean geometry. We don't live on a flat plane. We live in curved space, and we travel by geodesic, that is, the shortest possible line between two points on a curved surface. Newton interpreted gravity as the result of some attractive force, while Einstein defined it as the curvature of space-time.

Whenever physicists find a force, they look for a particle that creates and explains that force. Gravity is still largely a mystery, and particle physicists have spent a great deal of money hunting for gravity waves and their accompanying particle, the graviton.

Gravity waves are small ripples in space-time caused by large gravitational events. Einstein predicted gravity waves in 1915, but actually detecting them was a trick. Astrophysicists expected to find gravity waves rippling through space-time from supernovae and neutron stars and black holes, and they finally succeeded in detecting them on September 14, 2015, a century after Einstein predicted their existence. Twin Laser Interferometer Gravitational-wave Observatory (LIGO) detectors in Livingston, LA and Hanford, Washington used interferometers to hunt for gravity waves, and their success was a huge event for particle physicists everywhere.

Scientists are still hunting for gravitons – particles that are assumed to account for gravity. These massless, uncharged particles are presumably moving at the speed of light, but so far they have not been detected.

Science is the search for true answers about the nature of reality. People often do not realize, however, that the scientific method is actually the hunt for failures. Scientists make observations: they collect data based on patterns they see. They make a hypothesis, and then they go through the process of testing that hypothesis. The best way to test a hypothesis, however, is to try to *disprove* it. If a hypothesis triumphs over efforts to prove it wrong, then it reinforces its credibility. It's easy to create a bad theory based on a hypothesis somebody only tried to prove correct. It's in overcoming efforts to make it fail that we can formulate strong theories.

The process of testing a theory never ends, though, because a theory can never be proven. There is always the possibility that additional observations will show a theory's weaknesses and that adjustments will have to be made. Theories grow increasingly credible the more they resist being disproved, but theories can never be thoroughly proven. They are merely made stronger by time and testing.

Verifying Meaning

Claude Shannon was an electrical engineer who started revolutionizing computing in the 1930s. He was one of those genius innovators known for odd habits, like riding his unicycle down the research hallways at night while juggling. He notably applied Boolean logic to electrical switches, developing our system of zeroes and ones that became the nervous system of computing today. He went on to work for Bell Laboratories, where he worked on error-correcting communication systems and code making.

Shannon also stressed the importance of verifiability in the determination of meaning.

What does that mean, "determination of meaning"? Let's say that Grandma claims there are gnomes in the garden, but she herself has never seen them. What's more, when we go look for them, we can't see any either. Grandma tells us, "They turn invisible when you look for them."

There's no sense in Grandma's claim about the gnomes. There has to be some way of verifying the existence of the gnomes, otherwise Grandma's claims are meaningless. Maybe there are gnomes, and maybe there aren't. We can't determine anything about gnomes nobody can see. Claude Shannon declared that statements must be verifiable. We can't prove Grandma's gnome claims, but we can't disprove them either, and Shannon would have therefore categorized her statements as meaningless.

One of the primary rules in scientific investigation is that claims must be falsifiable. That is, there must be a way to test them and either show them to be true or false. One of the great tragedies of science is the slaying of a beautiful theory by an ugly fact. It can be a real heart breaker, but scientists have to be careful not to behave like Grandma. If there are inconvenient facts that don't fit a theory, scientists must be careful to avoid explaining away the problems. Problems are evidence too. Scientists need to keep testing, and they need to purge out wrong ideas. Hypotheses that cannot be tested – that are not falsifiable – are non-scientific. Holding onto them is intellectually dishonest.

The Scientific Method

Science is all about answering questions. What is the healthiest way to eat an egg? Does chocolate cure cancer? Why is the sky blue? The scientific method works well for most questions we have in today's world. There are certain steps that must be taken:

1) Ask a question.
2) Make observations / do background research.
3) Create a hypothesis.
4) Test the hypothesis through experiments.
5) Analyze the data and make conclusions.
6) Communicate the results.
7) Repeat.

Of course, it's important that the researchers do a good job of developing their hypotheses and the designs of their experiments, but the scientific method works to find answers to our daily questions.

However, when we ask questions about the distant past, we are in a difficult position. We have to fill in a huge puzzle picture with only a few of the pieces we need. Large chunks are missing, and we try to color in the rest of the picture with scattered pieces of information. When cosmologists ask, "What happened 100 billion years ago?" they face a mighty challenge. After all, they don't even know if there was a "100 billion years ago." Cosmologists make a variety of calculations based on certain assumptions and they argue that the universe is 13.8 billion years old, but they don't really know for certain.

They can't formally use the scientific method, because they can't run experiments on the past. They have to use the deductive method.

The Deductive Method

Through the deductive method, researchers create theories from generalizations about the universe. One deep thinker might develop a generalization that seems acceptable, and the rest of the thinkers derive theories from it. They then work to create experiments or find evidence that supports or tears apart their theory.

Basic logic is built on the deductive method. In order for a logical argument to be sound, it must follow two basic rules: a) its premises must be true and b) the structure of the argument must be valid. For instance. We can set up an argument:

> All A are B, and
> All B are C, therefore
> All A are C.

The structure of this deductive argument is valid, but what we put in for A and B and C determines whether the whole argument is sound. For instance, the following is nonsense.

> All clocks are tribbles, and
> All tribbles are bad tempered, therefore
> All clocks are bad tempered.

The problem here is that both premises are incorrect. Clocks are not tribbles, and tribbles are fictional cooing, snuggling little creatures that are not bad tempered at all. The final conclusion that all clocks are therefore bad tempered is completely silly.

On the other hand, we can find an argument in which both of the premises are true, but the argument is problematic because the structure is invalid:

> Some children like dark chocolate.
> Savannah is a child.
> Savannah likes dark chocolate.

The conclusion is not sound. Some children do like dark chocolate, and we can determine that Savannah is, in fact, a child, but we can't be sure about her particular position. She might hate dark chocolate. She might love dark chocolate, but we cannot determine her dark chocolate preferences from the structure of the argument.

Arguments are sound when both premises are true and the argument has a valid structure:

> All chickens are birds.
> All birds are warm blooded.
> All chickens are warm blooded.

> Only males have a Y-chromosome.
> Some children in Mrs. Martin's class
>   have a Y-chromosome.
> Some children in Mrs. Martin's class
>   are males.

In the discipline of logic, there are a string of fallacies – arguments that should be shunned. One is *Argumentum ad Ignorantiam* – the argument from ignorance. It is nonsense to say that something must be true just because we haven't proven it false. It's fallacious to say:

> *Nobody can give evidence that gnomes don't run around Grandma's garden. Therefore, gnomes must run around Grandma's garden.*

We can't demonstrate that gnomes don't run around Grandma's garden, but that doesn't mean they *do*. Human beings have a tendency to make this argument without realizing it, and it's a serious error.

The Struggles of Scientists

In deductive reasoning, a certain generalization can come in the form of mathematical proofs. That's a big one. Mathematicians work out elegant consistencies within a synthetic universe. These man-made mathematics are sometimes called the man-made universe. They define certain symbols and then they define how those symbols relate to each other:

A = 2B and
B = 2C therefore
A = 4C

These mathematical relationships can be useful. As different mathematicians get involved, they derive elegant models from the relationships. Models are used to make predictions that can be used to test theories. But, predictions might work in one domain and not another. If the predictions are found true, that gives support, and if the predictions don't work, then that discredits the theory. However, mathematicians have to be careful that their elegant models actually fit the real world. Many times a model will match reality for certain situations but not for others.

For instance, there are rules about the universe that apply to the physics of the baseball field but don't apply to the world inside the atom. Newtonian mechanics and quantum physics require different sets of equations, because atomic particles behave differently than baseballs. The point is that we can make extremely elegant mathematical models, but reality doesn't care how elegant they are. Some of the most brilliant minds on the planet have developed beautiful mathematical models, but that doesn't mean those models reflect the real world out there. Once the models are created, they have to be tested by making predictions that either come true – or don't – over and over again.

How did the universe begin? That's a good question. Cosmologists have told us that all the matter in the universe exploded into existence about 13.8 billion years ago in an event known as the Big Bang. The redshift of light from distant galaxies makes it appear that these galaxies are flying away from us at great speeds – an intergalactic Doppler effect. This implies that all the galaxies were once closer together at one point. In fact, most cosmologists believe all the matter in the universe was compressed into a space about the diameter of a dime before "kaboom!" It's the simplistic story about what happened in our past.

The reality is that a lot of ugly data go through astrophysicist labs – data that don't fit the pretty model. The farther we look into the universe, the farther back in time we go (because it took longer for the light to get here). Yet, no matter how deep we look, we still find large, mature, fully formed galaxies. Near the beginning of the universe, we'd have expected to see young galaxies still in the process of development. We also find that the Cosmic Background Radiation is clumped-up. We'd have expected it to be symmetrical and evenly spread out in all directions from the inflation that is said to have occurred at the beginning of the Big Bang. The CBR is anything but symmetrical and isotropic. There are a variety of other problems as well. For instance, we have not found the expected amount of lithium in the universe, and it gets worse as we look at the oldest stars.

In the 1970s, University of Arizona astronomer William Tifft started noticing "redshift periodicity." Tifft has spent 40 years collecting data on aberrant redshifts – which raises problems for the idea of a Big Bang and an expanding universe. Some light wave data indicate there are stars flying at us, first of all. Tifft also discovered that the redshift of star clusters comes at us in stair steps – in jumps – rather than in a smooth sloping manner. This told Tifft that the redshift was *not* a Doppler effect, as interpreted by most cosmologists. It had to be something else.

Two scientists at the Edinburgh Observatory were skeptical of Tifft's ideas about the stair-stepping redshift. Bruce Guthrie and William Napier set to work challenging Tifft's ideas, but in the end they confirmed that Tifft was correct about the redshift. If the redshift was digital, though, that meant it wasn't caused by the Doppler effect. Something else was going on.

Back in 1888, the Swedish physicist Johannes Rydberg developed a way to determine which chemical elements were out in space by studying the wavelengths of their spectral lines. Spectral lines are like thumbprints, and astrophysicists can use these spectral thumbprints to determine which elements a star contains, because the pattern is different for magnesium than it is for helium. The figure below shows the spectral lines from hydrogen, shown on a logarithmic scale some people call the Bar Codes of the Atom.

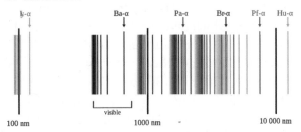

Rydberg had no way of knowing why different elements gave different spectral patterns, but we now understand that spectral lines are due to the movement of electrons between energy levels of an atom, and each element has its own unique pattern.

If the redshift changed according to step-by-step quantum levels, that would correspond to discrete *atomic* levels, which would be derived from the speed of light changing.

There's plenty of evidence that the speed of light has been changing over the ages. The universe might not be expanding at all; it might simply appear that way because of the deterioration of the speed of light itself. Australian physicists Barry Setterfield and Trevor Norman outlined the evidence for a decreasing speed of light in their 1987 paper "Atomic Constants, Light, and Time." Then, in 1999, Andreas Albrecht and João Magueijo suggested that a once-faster speed of light explained a number of problems in theoretical physics.

Astronomer Halton C. Arp worked at Hale Observatories in Southern California for 29 years, and his experience documenting unusual galaxies caused him to eventually challenge the Big Bang theory. He used a 200-inch telescope on Palomar Mountain to explore the night sky, and he collected information on oddities, cataloguing them in his *Atlas of Peculiar Galaxies* (1966). He found that celestial objects that appeared to be connected had radically different redshifts, which indicated that the redshifts had causes other than the Doppler effect. Certain quasars looked like they had been shot out of nearby spiral galaxies, and yet they had much larger redshifts than their galaxy progenitors. This caused Arp to conclude that the redshifts weren't just caused by velocity. He began to argue that the Big Bang theory was in error, which eventually led to his rejection by the astronomical community. His 1989 book *Quasars, Redshifts and Controversies* explains his journey.

Yet, despite growing problems with the Big Bang theory, the majority of astrophysicists still hold onto the model while offering explanations that excuse the failed predictions and significant difficulties.

Peer review hasn't helped the problem. Scientific research journals use peer review to evaluate new articles for publication. This allows the experts in the field to judge new research for its merits and ensure that shoddy work doesn't get published. However, it also puts a bit of a muzzle on those with unorthodox ideas. Peer reviewers can disparage new research that contradicts their own theoretical preferences. They can encourage the dispersion of some ideas or shut down others. In a perfect world, peer reviewers would be completely wise and would always value knowledge and innovation – but prejudices are as prevalent in academia as anywhere else. Old ideas can linger long past their shelf lives because of mental ossification in the universities. It's hard to teach old dogs new tricks, and those who hold to the respected, mainline viewpoints on certain issues are more likely to be published in peer-reviewed journals than those who challenge the scientific orthodoxy.

The nobility of the Bereans is valuable in all disciplines and not just theology. In Acts 17:11, Luke tells us that the Bereans were noble because they *"...received the Word with all readiness of mind, and searched the scriptures daily, whether those things were so."* In other words, they were willing to hear the new ideas that Paul preached, but they also were careful to research and test whether what Paul said was true. They weren't hard, unmoving cynics, but they also were not gullible sheep. That's a careful balance we all need to achieve. We need to keep our minds open enough to allow in the truth, whatever it is, but not so open that all our brains fall out.

The Illusion of Knowledge

The most certain barrier to truth is the conviction that we already have it. It's a problem that pervades in certain professional fields. As historian Daniel J Boorstin said so well, "The greatest obstacle to discovery is not ignorance – it is the illusion of knowledge."

Metaphors reign where mysteries reside. When we don't understand something, so often we give it an elegant name or an anecdotal association, and we allow the metaphor to take the place of true analysis. And so, metaphors reign where mysteries reside.

Science and technology. What is the difference between these?

Technology creates useful products from the information scientists discover. Quantum physics is a branch of science, but innovative individuals have used the discoveries of quantum physics to produce computers and cell phones. We can make a long list of incredible inventions that have been created in the past 50 years – astonishing advances in technology.

The advance of technology doesn't concern itself with the creation of the universe, with philosophical questions of who we are and why we're here. It doesn't dabble too much in the big questions of life. Technology is all about what works and what doesn't work. How do we create faster, smaller microprocessors? How do we get better definition and less pixilation from our digital cameras? What is the best way to get cell phone coverage into the little valleys of the Rocky Mountains – or the Alps? These are the questions of technology.

Science, on the other hand, has become a religion with a priesthood. It's not supposed to be. It's supposed to be about knowledge and discovery and the scientific method. Yet, in our world today, science has sought to answer the big questions of life once answered by religion. Who are we? Where did we come from? Why are we here? If scientists could answer these questions with a complete array of evidence, that would be one thing. Instead, we find that secular scientists have filled in the gaps of the vast picture puzzle with their own philosophies of the universe, and they ignore the evidence when it no longer fits their worldviews.

John Godfrey Saxe (1816-1887) took a famous Indian fable and made it into a charming little poem. I know we've used it before, but I've always enjoyed it since I read it as a kid. I think it gives us a view not just of theological wars, but of scientific wars as well.

The Blind Men and the Elephant

It was six men of Indostan,
To learning much inclined,
Who went to see the Elephant
(Though all of them were blind),
That each by observation
Might satisfy his mind.

The First approach'd the Elephant,
And happening to fall
Against his broad and sturdy side,
At once began to bawl:
"God bless me! but the Elephant
Is very like a wall!"

The Second, feeling of the tusk,
Cried, -"Ho! what have we here
So very round and smooth and sharp?
To me 'tis mighty clear,
This wonder of an Elephant
Is very like a spear!"

The Third approach'd the animal,
And happening to take
The squirming trunk within his hands,
Thus boldly up and spake:
"I see," -quoth he- "the Elephant
Is very like a snake!"

The Fourth reached out an eager hand,
And felt about the knee:
"What most this wondrous beast is like
Is mighty plain," -quoth he,-
"'Tis clear enough the Elephant
Is very like a tree!"

The Fifth, who chanced to touch the ear,
Said – "E'en the blindest man
Can tell what this resembles most;
Deny the fact who can,
This marvel of an Elephant
Is very like a fan!"

The Sixth no sooner had begun
About the beast to grope,
Then, seizing on the swinging tail
That fell within his scope,
"I see," -quoth he,- "the Elephant
Is very like a rope!"

And so these men of Indostan
Disputed loud and long,
Each in his own opinion
Exceeding stiff and strong,
Though each was partly in the right,
And all were in the wrong!

MORAL

So, oft in theologic wars
[I'll add physics wars here, too]
The disputants, I ween,
Rail on in utter ignorance
Of what each other mean;
And prate about an Elephant
Not one of them has seen!

Chapter 5
Milestones of Influence

Copernicus and Galileo laid out the evidence that the Earth and other planets flew around the Sun, overturning Ptolemy's centuries-old geocentric model of the solar system. A number of other scientists followed them, adding to our understanding of the solar system and the greater universe. Thick volumes could be dedicated to describing the astronomical discoveries of these subsequent scientists, but we will have to limit ourselves here to a few significant characters.

Johannes Kepler (1571-1630)

Kepler made a huge impact on the discipline of astronomy through his laws of planetary motion. Aristotle had portrayed the universe as a place of perfect circular orbits with the Earth at the center. Copernicus and Galileo upset the idea that all celestial bodies circled the Earth, but it was Kepler who realized that the planets made an elliptical pattern around the Sun. The great Danish astronomer Tycho Brahe had been taking notes on the movement of Mars, and as Kepler analyzed this data, he realized that Mars didn't make a circular orbit at all; it made an ellipse. In 1605,

Kepler's First Law declared that the planets made elliptical orbits around the Sun.

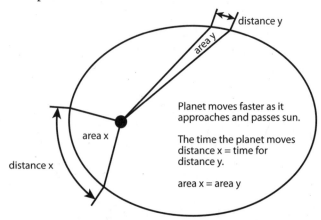

Planet moves faster as it approaches and passes sun.

The time the planet moves distance x = time for distance y.

area x = area y

Kepler also noted in his Second Law that the planets moved faster as they approached the Sun, so that the vector of movement always swept an equal area in an equal time. In other words, if the planet was far from the Sun, it traveled slower, and if were close to the Sun, it traveled faster. Because of this, the triangular shape made by the vector of distance-from-Sun and distance-traveled always had an equal area. In 1609, Kepler published these two laws in his book *Astronomia Nova*.

It took another 10 years for Kepler to publish his Third Law in *Harmonices Mundi*. On May 15, 1618, Kepler discovered a mathematical relationship between the planets' distances from the Sun and the time it took for them to orbit. It took much longer for planets to orbit the Sun when they were farther away. He stated that "the squares of the periodic times are to each other as the cubes of the mean distances," more simply written $P^2 \propto R^3$. This last law led Isaac Newton to his understanding of gravity far more than any falling apple.

Isaac Newton (1643-1727)

An object in motion stays in motion until it's acted on by an outside force.

Many people don't realize that Isaac Newton was a serious Christian who wrote commentaries on both Daniel and Revelation. He gave us both differential and integral calculus and made valuable advances in the exploration of optics. Newton was fascinated by God's creation, and his descriptions of classical mechanics have held for the greater part of three centuries. Einstein's theories of relativity trump Newton's mechanics as objects approach the speed of light, but Newton still stands strong in our day-to-day world. One of Newton's most important contributions, however, was his Law of Universal Gravitation.

According to Newton, gravity is caused by the attraction that bodies have on one another. Bodies with a large mass exert a strong pull and bodies with small mass exert a small pull, and the closer the bodies are together, the greater the magnitude of their attraction. Either way, the Earth pulls on us, and we pull on the Earth. The Earth pulls on the Moon, and the Moon pulls on the Earth, and this mutual attraction holds the two celestial bodies together.

Gravity applies to an infinite distance, but distance does weaken it exponentially. The force of gravity is proportional to the product of the two masses divided by the square of their distance from each other. This is called the inverse-square law of gravitation:

$$F \propto \frac{m1 * m2}{d^2}$$

Because the gravitational force diminishes according to the square of the distance between two objects, the impact of gravity on the universe appears to be highly overrated by astrophysicists today. Electromagnetism is a much more powerful force than gravity when great distances are involved.

Ben Franklin (1706-1790)

We generally think of Ben Franklin as a statesman and an important contributor to the American Revolution and new U.S. government. His hobby of inventing things isn't always appreciated as much as it should be. Yes, he invented the pot belly stove and bifocals, and yes he toyed with electricity by flying a key on a kite string, but we don't recognize the value of his role as an innovator.

Franklin believed that the lightning seen during thunderstorms was a form of electricity, and his June 1752 kite string experiment determined that the sky was inherently electrical in nature. He also believed that electricity flowed like a fluid, and he invented the lightning rod to direct lightning from the tops of barns to the ground so that the barns would not catch fire. This discovery that we can harness and direct the flow of electricity has become supremely important to modern civilization. Franklin did not invent electricity, of course, but he invented many of the terms we still use today in describing the flow and storage of electricity, including "positive" and "negative" charges, "battery" and "conductor."

Michael Faraday (1791-1867)

Albert Einstein kept a photograph of Michael Faraday on the wall of his study alongside those of Newton and James Clerk Maxwell, and the honor was well-deserved. Faraday was a genius with both electromagnetic fields and chemistry, and he can be considered one of the most important scientists of all time. I could write chapters on his accomplishments alone. He jump-started the study of electromagnetism by his experiments on magnetic fields produced around conductors carrying direct current. He showed that changing a magnetic field created an electric field; he created one of the first electric motors called a homopolar motor; and, he showed that magnetism affects light. He also produced a variety of other beneficial additions to science, like the Bunsen burner and a system of oxidation numbers used commonly by today's chemists. Capacitance (the ability of a capacitor to hold electricity) is measured today in "farads" in honor of Faraday.

Many scientists like Newton and Max Planck were dedicated Christians. Some of the greatest minds in history were God-fearing people. They might have had different doctrinal perspectives, but they were God-fearing people. Faraday was also highly religious and served as a member of a Christian sect that demanded total faith and commitment. Biographers have noted that "a strong sense of the unity of God and nature pervaded Faraday's life and work." The Faraday Institute for Science and Religion was founded in his honor in 2006 to carry out academic research and improve the public's understanding of the interaction between science and religion.

James Clerk Maxwell (1831-1879)

Einstein is considered perhaps the greatest mind of the 20th century, and yet Einstein owed a great deal of his own enlightenment to the equations of James Clerk Maxwell. Maxwell's self-consistent equations codified the basis of all electrical science and engineering. He developed the classical theory of electromagnetic radiation that tied together electricity, magnetism and light as different manifestations of the same substance. He proposed that electromagnetic energy propagates through empty space, which led to the prediction of radio waves. His discoveries laid the foundation for 20th century physics, including special relativity, quantum mechanics, thermodynamics and even information theory and cybernetics. Einstein called Maxwell's work the "most profound and the most fruitful that physics has experienced since the time of Newton."

Maxwell's equations are four partial differential equations that relate the electric and magnetic fields to their sources, charge density, and current density. These equations can be combined to show that light is an electromagnetic wave.

William Thomson, 1st Baron Kelvin (1824-1907)

British scientist William Thomson is better known by his title: Lord Kelvin. He is famous for calculating absolute zero as -273.15°C. He was knighted for his work on thermodynamics, but he was an outspoken critic and pessimist about the future of electricity and electromagnetic theory. He felt that radio and wireless telegraphy had no future. He was an influential man but he took a position against electromagnetism and, as a result, the whole British scientific establishment tended to ignore Maxwell for a time.

Modeling the Universe

Astronomer Robert Burnham ran the Lowell Observatory from 1950 to 1979. During this time, he developed a *Celestial Handbook* to help stargazers recognize and identify the multitude of objects in the night sky.

In his Handbook, Burnham proposes a model of the solar system. There are 63,360 inches in a statute mile, and Burnham noticed that there are about 63,240 astronomical units in one light year. (An astronomical unit is the distance between the Earth and the Sun.) This is a convenient coincidence, because it is much easier for us to understand inches and miles than it is to conceptualize a light year. This coincidence allows us to picture light years through space in terms of miles on Earth.

We can say there are *about* 63,300 inches in a mile and *about* 63,300 astronomical units per light year, and using this ratio, we can create a mental picture that helps us understand the vastness of the Universe. In our mind, one inch can represent the distance between the Earth and Sun, and one mile can represent the distance light travels in one year.

The Sun is about 880,000 miles in diameter and it's about 93 million miles away from the Earth.

If one inch represents the distance between the Earth and the Sun in our model, then the diameter of the Sun looks like a small dot – about a hundredth of an inch. All the planets of our solar system would then be able to fit within a five-foot circle. They'd be too small to see (since the Sun itself is just a dot), but we can imagine that Mercury is 0.25 inches away from that speck of a Sun, and Venus is 0.70 of an inch away. The Earth, of course, is one inch away, and Mars is about 1.6 inches. Jupiter is a great leap to 5.2 inches and Saturn sits almost twice as far from the Sun as Jupiter at 9.5 inches. Uranus and Neptune are way *way* out there, at 19.2 and 30 inches respectively. In our model, the solar system from the Sun to Neptune has a radius of 30 inches, a diameter of five feet.

Our nearest solar neighbor is Alpha Centauri, a binary star system that is about twice the mass of our Sun. We are four and a half light years away from Alpha Centauri. Using the same ratio for our model, the double-speck of Alpha Centauri hangs in the Universe about four and a half miles away from the speck of our Sun.

That's an incredible distance. Gravity is a force with infinite range, but the force grows vastly weaker as the distance increases. According to Newton's Law of Universal Gravitation, the force between two objects is proportional to the mass of the first object times the mass of the second object, all divided by the *square* of the distance between the two objects:

$$F = G \frac{m_1 * m_2}{r^2}$$

This inverse-square law is extremely important. The force is influenced hugely by distance, because it's inversely proportional to the distance *squared*. The gravitational pull of our speck of a Sun affects the Earth at one inch away, and it even affects Neptune at 30 inches away. The force between two objects two inches apart is ¼ that of the same two objects when they are one inch apart. If the Earth were 30 times farther from the Sun, the gravitational attraction between the Sun and Earth would be $1/900^{th}$ what it is now. In other words, two specks of dust separated by four and a half miles will not know the other exists – and Alpha Centauri is our nearest neighbor. How much gravity can we expect two specks to feel when they are separated by 4.5 miles? Essentially none.

As we explore the variety of issues in this book, we recognize that many astronomers have presumed a gravitational universe. Gravity is useful for our solar system, because the distances are nominal. When we talk about the relationships between neighboring stars and galaxies, gravity becomes pretty unimportant. Most of the night sky is far beyond our gravitational touch.

It's interesting that while Lord Kelvin was disparaging electromagnetism, the Scandinavian scientists in Norway and Sweden were fascinated by auroras – the Northern Lights. They quickly realized that phenomena like the aurora borealis are electrical, which led them into the physics of plasmas. And plasmas make a much greater impact on the universe than gravity could ever dream...

Chapter 6
The Plasma Universe

*His going forth is from the end of the heaven,
and his circuit unto the ends of it.*

Psalm 19:6

Next time you walk past a bright neon sign, stop for a moment and look at it. The atoms inside the tube are in an excited plasma state. The electrons have separated from the nucleus of their atoms and are running free as a cloud of ions. Electricity flows through that plasma cloud, and the tube lights up orange or red or green.

We're familiar with three states of matter – solid, liquid and gas. Place an ice cube in a pan and set it on the stove. The slowly moving, crystallized water molecules have been locked together with hydrogen bonds. As heat enters the system, the hydrogen bonds start to break and the water molecules move more and more freely. Soon, the ice melts into liquid water. As the burner continues to cook under the pan, the heat gives increasing energy to the water molecules. Soon the water molecules break away from each other altogether and escape into the air as steam. The water has entered a gas phase.

Water below 32°F (0°C) freezes into a solid. At room temperature it is liquid, and above 212°F (100°C) it boils into steam that dissipates as a gas.

We understand solids, liquids and gasses because we experience them in our daily lives. We don't often deal with plasmas, the fourth state of matter. Yet, most of the matter in the universe is in the form of a plasma. If energy were added to those water molecules floating in the air, so much that the molecules broke apart and the electrons escaped their protons, a plasma cloud would be formed. Plasmas are highly ionized clouds filled with positive nuclei and free negative electrons. The cloud works as a single material, able to conduct electricity and magnetism. Gasses don't easily transmit electricity, but plasmas do.

The Power of Electromagnetism

The effects of electromagnetism can be 10^{39} times greater than the effects of gravity, yet the astronomical community continues to focus on gravity rather than on electromagnetism as the significant force in the universe. There are a variety of phenomena in the universe that should make us realize we need to place more emphasis on plasmas.

For instance, the search for "missing matter" in the universe. Scientists have been spending decades looking for "dark matter" to explain why the arms of spiral galaxies are spinning as fast as the cores of the galaxies. The galaxies should be flying apart if the outsides are moving so fast. Physicists have argued that unseen "dark matter" adds gravitational force that holds the galaxies together. Researchers have been hunting for dark matter for decades and have yet to find it. They argue that 96% of the universe is made of dark energy and dark matter – but they base this on assumptions about the universe that might not be correct.

The Andromeda galaxy, M31, is one of the most famous, beautiful things to see in the night sky. On the infrared, however, it's clear that electrical things are going on there. The starburst galaxy M82 is allegedly affected by gravitational tidal forces from neighboring M81. Both galaxies can be found in the Ursa Major constellation, but they are 300,000 light years from each other. Spiral galaxies are believed to all have supermassive black holes at their centers, around which the billions and trillions of stars swirl. M81 is said to have a black hole of 70 million M☉ (solar masses), and M82 a black hole of 30 million M☉.

We can quickly calculate the gravitational force between these two galaxies by applying Newton's inverse-square law. First we have to convert all the measurements into the correct units of meters and kilograms. "G" – the gravitational constant – has a value of about 6.7×10^{-11} N m^2/kg^2. There are approximately 9.5×10^{15} meters in a light year, so 300,000 light years would be 2.85×10^{21}m. One solar mass is about 2×10^{30} kg, which means that M81 has a mass of 1.4×10^{38} kg, and M82 has a mass of 6×10^{37} kg. To determine the gravitational force between these two galaxies, we can work out the following equation:

$$F = G \frac{m_1 * m_2}{r^2}$$

$$F \approx 6.7 \times 10^{-11} \left(\frac{N\,m^2}{kg^2}\right) \frac{(1.4 \times 10^{38} kg) \times (6 \times 10^{37} kg)}{(2.85 \times 10^{31} m)^2}$$

$$F \approx 7 \times 10^{22}\ N.$$

The gravitational pull between these two galaxies is therefore about 7×10^{22} N. To get some perspective, the force that the Sun and Earth exert on each other is about 3.5×10^{22} N. This means that the force between the fantastically massive galaxies of M81 and M82 is only about 2x as great as the gravitational force between the relatively puny specks of the Sun and the Earth, and we're not even counting the full distances to the centers of each galaxy. This gives us a picture of the inadequacy of gravity as an interstellar or intergalactic force. As we look at these galaxies through different wavelengths of light, however, we realize there are *electromagnetic* forces at work. Pulsars are spinning neutron stars that send out pulses of electromagnetic radiation. A variety of celestial objects are connected electrically and magnetically – not gravitationally.

Remember our four fundamental forces: the strong and weak nuclear forces, the electromagnetic force and the gravitational force. The strong force is the strongest of the four, but it has a limited range; it doesn't reach past the nucleus of an atom. The gravitational force has an infinite range, but it is 10^{38} times weaker than the strong force. The electromagnetic force also has an infinite range, and it is just 100 times weaker than the strong force – or 10^{36} times *stronger* than gravity. What's more, the electromagnetic force can act both positively and negatively. It can attract and it can repulse. Once we start dealing with large distances, gravity evaporates into irrelevancy. Electromagnetism is what it's all about, but for some reason its significance has been largely overlooked by the field of astronomy. However, there have been a few bright minds who brought plasmas to our attention, and just as we have appreciated the contributions of Kant, Newton and Maxwell, it's valuable to tip our hats to those who taught us about plasmas.

The Fathers of Plasma

Kristian Birkeland (1867-1917)

While the British largely ignored electromagnetism, those in Scandinavian countries watched the polar auroras with fascination. We now know that auroras are caused by the collisions of charged particles, like electrons, in the Earth's magnetosphere at high altitudes. The Norwegian researcher Kristian Birkeland is called the "father of plasma experiments" for his work on plasmas, both in the laboratory and in space. He is a legend in this field. He made treks to the Norwegian polar region to study the aurora displays, and he was the first to recognize that electric currents flow from the sun to excite plasmas in the Earth's upper atmosphere.

Birkeland predicted the existence of twisted, corkscrew-shaped high intensity currents in plasmas now called Birkeland currents. They follow magnetic fields rather than cut across them. He was nominated for the Nobel Prize in physics seven times, and his portrait remains on the Norwegian 200 Kroner currency note to this day.

Irving Langmuir (1881-1957)

Irving Langmuir was an American physical chemist who won the 1932 Nobel Prize in chemistry "for his discoveries and investigations in surface chemistry." He did research for the General Electric Company at Schenectady, New York, and his work on filaments led to the gas-filled incandescent lamp. It was Langmuir who coined the term "plasma" and he invented what are called Langmuir probes still used today.

Langmuir discovered the electrostatic double layer in plasmas. He described the almost lifelike self-organizing behavior of these ionized clouds in the presence of electric currents and magnetic fields when foreign objects are inserted into them. When a foreign body is placed in a plasma cloud, it surrounds it and creates what's called a Debye sheath. The electrons are lighter and faster, and they shoot out of the plasma onto the surface of the object. A layer of positive ions will then gather atop the electrons to balance the negative charge built up on the material of the foreign body. This double layer of electrons and positive ions – this Debye sheath – creates a transition from the plasma to the solid object surface, and it's the strongest electric field in any plasma. Langmuir worked with this double layer, and he invented a probe that was able to measure what was going on inside the Debye sheath. It's a very clever device.

Hannes Alfvén (1908-1995)

One of the biggest originators of plasma cosmology was Hannes Alfvén, who also happened to win the 1970 Nobel Prize in physics for his work on magnetohydrodynamics.

In 1963, Alfvén was the first to predict the largescale filamentary structure of the universe. He also first proposed the mechanism for the acceleration of cosmic rays – now known as the Fermi mechanism. In 1966, Alfvén published

Worlds-Antiworlds, and in 1981 he published *Cosmic Plasma*. The Alfvén-Klein cosmology states that matter and antimatter fill the universe in equal amounts, but what amount to Debye sheaths form boundaries between the regions of matter and antimatter; double layers of opposite charges form cosmic electromagnetic fields that generate enough radiation to form plasmas.

There has long been a question among particle physicists about why there happens to be more matter than antimatter in the universe – why there aren't equal amounts that annihilate each other. Alfvén's model argues there are equal amounts, but in pockets, and we happen to live in a pocket that contains more matter than antimatter.

Anthony Peratt (1940-)

Following the leads of Birkeland and Alfvén, modern-day cosmologist Anthony Peratt has continued to develop a cosmology based on plasmas rather than gravity. Peratt has worked at a variety of labs, including stints as a guest scientist at both the Max Planck Institute for Physics and Astrophysics in Germany and the Alfvén Laboratory of the Royal Institute of Technology in Sweden. He has served in the Applied Theoretical Physics Division at Los Alamos National Laboratory since 1981.

Peratt took advantage of terawatt generators to create plasmas at Los Alamos. He then created models of the plasmas in the greater universe based on what was gleaned about plasmas in the laboratory. He studied double-radio galaxies and discovered that his computer simulations matched what astronomers found in those galaxies – that different galaxy forms represented the same material at different ages of development. His simulations suggest that radio galaxies are the precursors of all other kinds of galaxies. In 1992, he published a book called *The Physics of the Plasma Universe*, which emphasizes the relevance of plasma in astrophysical models – for instance, in explaining magnetic fields and cosmic rays.

In a 1989 article, Peratt states:
Our satellites and spacecraft have discovered what we once thought of as empty space is rather a dynamic sea of low-density charged particles, called plasma...this sea is traversed by electric and magnetic fields and is filled with complex flow patterns and electric currents transporting and depositing energy over large distances...

If plasmas are found throughout the solar system, then what of the rest of the cosmos? For those oriented to seeing plasmas, the cosmos is filled with demonstrations of plasma behavior, and astronomical observation substantiates that more than 99 percent of the matter in the universe exists in the plasma state...

The differences in content of the Big Bang model and the Plasma Universe model reflect a…fundamental methodological difference. Following the traditional theoretical mode of modern general relativity and particle physics, the Big Bang model attempts to deduce and explain observations of the universe beginning from original principles. This contrasts with the attempt by the Plasma Universe model to replicate much of the measured extragalactic data in astrophysics based on experimental and simulational investigations.

While the Big Bang model remains the respected cosmological model, interest in the role of magnetic fields in galaxies has grown. In the meanwhile, Peratt has done research on fusion power and the z-pinch effect, which creates magnetic fields that "pinch" or confine the very plasmas used to create the fields. He went on to work as an advisor to the U.S. Department of Energy (1995-1999) and has since turned to archeology, combing through prehistoric rock art for evidences of space plasma events in ancient times.

In chapters 38-41 of Job, God gives Job a science quiz, challenging him on a variety of aspects of the natural world. In Job 38:31, God asks, *"Canst thou bind the sweet influences of Pleiades, or loose the bands of Orion?"*

We can quickly do some calculations and discover the stars that make up the Pleiades are too far apart from each other for gravity to be responsible for binding them together. In fact, the Pleiades are known as an "unbound" star cluster, and the stars are expected to eventually fly away from each other if enough time permits. On the other hand, the four bright stars of Orion's belt – the Trapezium – are at the front of a huge dust cloud. The Orion Nebular Cluster is a bound cluster, with the Trapezium Cluster at its core. X-rays pour from a powerful plasma bubble in the Orion Nebula. God is challenging Job. Who do you think you are? Can you bind the Pleiades together? Can you loosen the bands of Orion? No. Job knew nothing about plasmas *or* gravity. He knew nothing about the connection of stars in the cosmos or how God held the constellations in the sky.

In Genesis 1, we find the strange description of the "firmament" - רָקִיעַ - *raqiya`* in Hebrew. We are told that this mysterious expanse separated the waters above from the waters below. The Hebrew word for "waters" is מַיִם - *mayim*. Could those waters include plasmas? I'm just throwing that out. I don't know.

Maxwell's Equations

As a set, these laws describe classical electromagnetism, and astrophysicists have unfortunately tended to ignore them. Individually, they are known as follows:

1. $\nabla \cdot D = \rho_v$
2. $\nabla \cdot B = 0$
3. $\nabla \times E = -\dfrac{\partial B}{\partial t}$
4. $\nabla \times H = \dfrac{\partial D}{\partial t} + J$

1. Gauss' Law
2. Gauss' Law for magnetism
3. Faraday's Law of induction
4. Ampere's Law with Maxwell's correction

Maxwell imagined electric and magnetic fields to be like flowing liquid. Liquid comes from a source, like a spout, and it flows toward a destination, like the hole in the bottom of a sink. The upside-down triangle with the dot is the "divergence" operator, which tells us whether a field is flowing out or in, whether it acts as a source or as a sink in space. The upside-down triangle with the x – the "curl" operator – tells us the field curls in a small circle.

Gauss' Law describes how an electric field behaves around electrical charges. If there's no electrical charge in a system, the divergence of D (the electric flux density) is 0. There is no flow. However, if there is a charge, then the total electric flux leaving any volume of space is equal to the total charge inside that volume.

D	= the electric flux density
E	= the electric field
H	= the magnetic field
B	= μH (μ = permeability)
J	= current density [current per unit of area]
ρ_v	= charge density [charge per unit of volume]
$\delta/\delta t$	= change with respect to time.
$\nabla\cdot$	= the divergence operator in vector calculus
$\nabla\times$	= the curl operator in vector calculus

The second law applies to magnetism rather than electric flux. Since there is no such thing as magnetic charge, the divergence of the magnetic field is always zero. All magnets are dipoles – with a negative end and a positive end. Magnetic monopoles don't exist, and so there is no "magnetic charge" and no divergence.

We don't need to keep going. Maxwell started off exploring electricity and magnetism and he ended up discovering that light was an electromagnetic wave travelling at approximately 300,000 kilometers per second.

There are some interesting things to note about magnetic fields. For instance, the forces are orthogonal to the fields. That is, the force exerted on a moving charge by a magnetic field is 90° from the movement of field itself. It's easy to think that the force would happen in the direction the field is moving, but instead, the force is perpendicular. Engineers quickly learn what's called the right hand rule – if you stick your index finger in the

direction of the charge's
velocity, your other fingers
will curl outward in the
direction of the magnetic
field, and your thumb will
stick upward in the direction
of the magnetic force.

Another right-hand rule can tell you the
direction of a magnetic field around a wire that's
carrying current. If you wrap your fingers in a
semi-circle around a wire, with your thumb in the
direction that the current is flowing, your fingers
will curl in the direction of the magnetic field.

The Modes of Plasma

Plasma actually operates in three different
modes:

The Dark Current Mode: In this mode,
the plasma does not glow because the current
is too low. This makes it essentially invisible.
The magnetospheres of the planets are plasmas
in dark current mode. We have to measure the
electrical activity of these plasmas to know they
exist at all.

The Earth's ionosphere is a dark current plasma,
which only becomes visible during an aurora event.
The ionosphere allows us to send radio waves
around the world. We know that light is bent
when it moves from air to water; it's refracted as it

changes from a faster medium to a slower medium. Radio waves also bend when they are sent from the Earth into space, because they are refracted as they go through the ionosphere. Yet, we cannot see the ionosphere with our eyes, because the electrical current flowing through it is so low.

Normal Glow Mode: As the strength of the electrical current increases through a plasma, the electrons get excited and collide with each other, generating photons so that the plasma begins to glow visibly. The brightness of that glow depends on how intense the current is, whether in a neon light on a barroom wall or in a Northern Lights display. The color of the glow depends on the particular gas being ionized. The Sun's corona is a glow-mode plasma discharge. It only exists because the Sun is electrical in nature, and ions flow from the Sun's surface, through the corona and out into the open galaxy as a solar "wind."

Arc Mode: The electrical current running through plasma can get so high that the current forms twisting filaments. Think of arc welding – electric welding. We are taught immediately to protect our eyes and avoid watching while somebody is doing electric welding, because the brightness of that light will ruin eyes. A plasma in arc mode produces a wide range of electromagnetic radiation – from ultraviolet to radio waves.

Birkeland Currents

Currents that follow magnetic field lines
are called Birkeland currents, and they were
originally associated with the auroras in the Earth's
ionosphere. As high-intensity electric currents
pass through a plasma, it can take on a corkscrew
or spiral shape, forming a filamental or cable-like
structure. These Birkeland currents are one of
the z-pinch phenomena, because the current is
pinched into the filamental cable by the magnetic
fields created by the current. Birkeland currents
often occur in pairs; those moving parallel in the
same direction are attracted to each other and
those moving in opposite directions repulse each
other (with an electromagnetic force proportional
to the inverse square of their distance, just like the
gravitational force, strangely enough.)

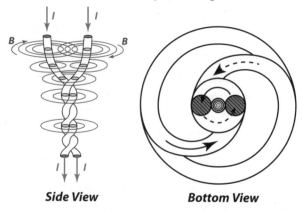

Side View   **Bottom View**

The cosmic matter we see out there tends
to form an abundance of filamentary stringy

structures due to Birkeland currents, all interacting with each other and producing interesting cosmic effects.

Now, remember that the initial velocity of a particle is perpendicular to its magnetic field. The path the particle takes is a circle in the plane perpendicular to that field. However, if the velocity of the particle is at an angle slightly different than 90 degrees to the magnetic field, the path will then be a helix or a spiral.

If Birkeland currents come in pairs, they'll twist themselves into a double helix – one that looks just like a cosmic double strand of DNA. In cosmic space, the plasma filaments can be observed by the electromagnetic radiation they emit. The radiation might not be in the range of visible light, but we can still measure it.

Marklund Convection

The cable of the Birkeland currents acts like an ion sump, which pulls ions out of nearby space into the area between the filaments. A process called the Marklund convection sorts the different chemical elements that have been pulled into the area of compression.[6] In other words, the hydrogen and helium, silicon and magnesium do not mix homogenously. They distribute themselves in rotating cylinders according to their ionization potentials. Helium collects on the outside with hydrogen as the next layer down. Nitrogen and oxygen form in the middle and metals like iron, silicon and magnesium form rings on the inside. This sorting mechanism is called the Marklund convection. We think of convection in terms of heat rising, but in plasma physics it has to do with ionization potentials – that is, the energy required to change a neutral atom into an ion by removing an electron.

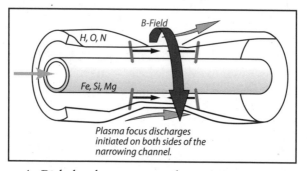

Plasma focus discharges initiated on both sides of the narrowing channel.

As Birkeland currents reach a certain proximity to each other, a repulsion force holds them apart. The double-spiral is quite stable, and extreme compression of matter can take place in the cylindrical space inside. Anything caught inside gets squeezed. As the charge density increases, certain spots can transition into a z-pinch, condensing matter into balls of plasma. It is thought that stars might be created in this fashion. If matter is squeezed from an ionized state to a solid state, planets might be formed. We believe that God created all the stars and planets and their moons on the Fourth Day of Creation, by His

Word. What did that look like? In Isaiah 45:12, God tells us, "*I have made the earth, and created man upon it: I, even my hands, have stretched out the heavens, and all their host have I commanded.*"

God stretched out the heavens and He calls all the stars by name.

Electric Currents in the Sun

The Sun is not just a ball of fire. It has different levels to it, starting at the center with its nuclear core, where fusion reactions are said to take place. Above the core is its radiative zone, followed by its convection zone, through which heat bubbles up. The surface of the Sun is called the photosphere, above which is the chromosphere – the Sun's atmosphere. As the chromosphere transitions to the corona, the temperature rises dramatically, which is surprising. We would think that the Sun's surface would be hot, and the atmosphere would grow cooler as we move farther out. Instead, the temperature rises logarithmically as we move out through the corona. Why? Because the Sun is electrical.[7]

We also find that the voltage inside the Sun is fairly steady, but as soon as we hit the chromosphere, the voltage drops like a cliff. An electrical engineer recognizes that this is almost identical to the profile of a transistor. The Sun is an electrical phenomenon.

Because it's electrical, the Sun has currents. We find that electrons enter the Sun at its poles and positive ions exit at its equator, forming currents. These moving, charged particles create a complex magnetic field. If the main current from each pole increases in strength, it creates secondary currents going the opposite direction and producing what amounts to a double layer between the arc mode of the photosphere and the glow mode of the corona. The magnetic field of the Sun is incredibly powerful, affecting charged particles beyond the distance of the known planets.

Why is this important? The Sun's current and its magnetic field don't remain steady and constant. There's a rise and fall, a strengthening and weakening at times, and if the current weakens, the secondary surface currents reverse direction, and ultimately the magnetic polarity of the Sun reverses. The direction of the current isn't what's important – it's all about whether it's increasing or decreasing in strength. We see these reversals taking place every 11 years, and that's why we have 11-year sun spot cycles.

Solar flares are caused electrically. A strong looping current will produce a secondary magnetic field that will surround and try to expand the loop. If the current becomes too strong, the double layer that contains it will be punctured. If the voltage gradient becomes strong enough, the discharge path will break. The energy stored in the primary magnetic field will be explosively released into space as a solar flare.

It's amazing how much of what we didn't understand about the sun suddenly does make sense because it's a plasma, and the sun is, in effect, a very sophisticated transformer. It draws energy from the fields it's passing through and converts that energy into a form of radiation that can be helpful to the planet Earth.

Chapter 7

Stretching the Heavens

Einstein's relativity gave us the common view of space-time as something physical and substantial. Astrophysicists talk about the "fabric of space-time." Yet, long before Einstein, the Bible writers described space as something physical, something that could be stretched and rolled up. Space can be:

Torn	Isaiah 64:1
Worn out like a garment	Psalm 102:25-26
Shaken	Isaiah 13:13; Haggai 2:6; Hebrews 12:26
Burnt up	2 Peter 3:12
Rolled up	Isaiah 34:4; Revelation 6:14

In Psalm 104:2, the heavens are described as a curtain that can be spread out. In Isaiah 40:22, God stretches out the heavens like a tent to live in. This idiom of the heavens behaving like fabric can be seen throughout the Bible, and it's an accurate description. We know that space can be warped and bent. The Bible says that space can be rolled up – which implies that there must be more than four dimensions, because there must be room for the four dimensions of space-time to roll up *in*. M-Theory predicts at least 10 dimensions (3+1+6). That is, there are the three dimensions of space and one dimension of time that we currently experience, plus six additional dimensions beyond our direct understanding.

Zero-Point Energy

In our minds, we often think of outer space as empty. It is, after all, the "vacuum of space." Yet, physicists have come to realize that there is incredible energy pervading every cubic centimeter of supposedly empty space.

From 1911 to 1913, Max Planck introduced the idea of a zero-point energy (ZPE), the underlying energy in the very fabric of the universe. This is the energy that still exists at a temperature of absolute zero – at 0 Kelvin. Even when every bit of heat is removed from a system, helium remains a liquid and refuses to freeze solid because its atoms are still moving around due to the ZPE.

In 1925, Robert S. Mulliken noticed that the wavelengths of spectral lines were shifted from their theoretical positions. He was among the first to recognize that the energy in space was battering atoms and affecting their movement. It became understood that Planck's constant was actually the measurement of the uncertainty in position of subatomic particles, and by 1960 it was realized that this uncertainty of position was caused by battering from the ZPE.

In 1987 Hal Puthoff showed that the electrons stayed in their orbits and did not go either spinning out or spinning in due to expended energy precisely because of the energy they received from the zero point energy.

Physicist Paul Davies estimates that the ZPE may be as much as 10^{110} joules per cubic centimeter of empty space.[8] That's a ridiculous amount of energy! If we could "tap" into it, we could eliminate all worries about whether we should use fossil fuels or renewable resources. Empty space itself would be the ultimate resource. Barry Setterfield used the following illustration to put this amount of power into perspective:

> *A bright light bulb radiates at 150 watts. By contrast, our sun radiates at 3.8 x 10^{26} watts. In our galaxy there are 100 billion stars. If they all radiate at about the same intensity as our sun, then the amount of energy expended by our entire galaxy of stars shining for 10 billion years is roughly the energy locked up in one cubic centimeter of space. The physical vacuum is not just an empty nothingness.[9]*

Unfortunately, we can't tap that energy, because it's evenly distributed all around us. We don't feel the 14.7 psi of air pressure pushing on us for the same reason – it's balanced by even distribution. Whether we feel it or not, ZPE is there, and an underlying energy pervades the universe around us.

The bottom line is that space has physical properties. Einstein showed us that energy and mass are different forms of the same stuff ($E=mc^2$), and space is filled with energy. Space has permittivity. It has permeability. It has an intrinsic impedance, which any amateur radio ham knows, because we have to tune our antennas to the impedance of space. These are engineering terms, but they all mean one thing: space has physical properties. It has properties of its own, properties that exist whether or not there are atoms in it.

Epistemology

The final frontier of all sciences are now the information sciences. At the boundaries of our reality is information. Quantum physics, Heisenberg's uncertainty, Schrödinger's cat – these ideas ultimately all have to do with information theory.

We often think of information theory in connection to ever-faster telecommunications and quantum computing, but it applies readily to the biological sciences. When we look at molecular biology or immunology or genetics, we quickly find that the cellular world is filled with coding and switches. We've discovered that DNA is a digital code with self-correcting mechanisms in place. Biologists cannot explain the origin of life because they can't explain the origin of information. Functional proteins have never spontaneously created themselves from random amino acids in a laboratory; they are coded for by DNA using a system of biological machinery that has a specific setup. DNA is reproduced in the cell by copying an existing template.

Where did the code come from in the first place? Secular biologists argue that intelligent design is not required as an explanation for life, and yet the systems found in every cell in our bodies cannot be duplicated in the outside world without research and development and blueprints and careful engineering.

Photosynthesis is a marvelous, miraculous process. It means "to build with light" and that's exactly what plants do. Green plants use sunlight to convert CO_2 into glucose, which is used by the plants for energy. Plants absorb CO_2 from the air through their stomata – little windows in their leaves – and from their stomata they also release the oxygen so important for animal life. The small, green sugar factories in the chloroplasts of green plants can produce millions of new glucose molecules each second. When the weather is friendly, plants produce more glucose than they use and store it in their roots, stems, and leaves in the form of starches and other carbohydrates. Animals can then eat these plants for their own energy needs, since animals cannot photosynthesize and produce their own glucose. Each year, photosynthesizing organisms produce about 170 billion metric tons of carbohydrates from sunlight and CO_2 in the air.[10] That's fantastic. That's about 25 metric tons for each human being on our planet.

Photosynthesis allows life on earth to exist, and biologists have a hard time explaining how it originated. "Simple" algae use photosynthesis, yet photosynthesis is not a simple process. It's complex and amazing, and it's ludicrous to suggest it just *appeared* in cyanobacteria early in Earth's evolutionary history with no further explanation.

It is foolish to attribute design and engineering to random processes. Randomness is, by definition, the absence of design. A child might take a bag of blocks and dump them on the ground over and over and at some point find that four or five land on top of each other, making what appears to be a pillar. However, a child will never dump out a bag of blocks on the ground and find they randomly build a replica of the Eiffel Tower.

In astrophysics we find that the fabric of space becomes an information issue. We are beginning to suspect that our universe is holographic in nature – a giant projection that merely reflects the existence of a deeper, truer reality.

Something More

When Adam and Eve disobeyed God and were cast out of the Garden, the entire world changed. Creation became subject to futility and bondage.[11] Even more disastrous, we were separated from God and no longer had the free access and personal conversations that Adam and Eve once enjoyed. To reveal Himself to us, however, the Creator has given us His Word. We trust that God's Word is pure,[12] especially since God puts His Word above His Name![13]

> *The law of the LORD is perfect, converting the soul: the testimony of the LORD is sure, making wise the simple. The statutes of the LORD are right, rejoicing the heart: the commandment of the LORD is pure, enlightening the eyes. The fear of the LORD is clean, enduring for ever: the judgments of the LORD are true and righteous altogether.*
>
> Psalm 19:7-9

What does the Bible say about the Creation? At the very beginning, Genesis 1:3, Moses tells us, "And *God said* 'let there be…'" God spoke, and what He *said* came to pass. Moses wasn't just some passing self-proclaimed prophet; God talked directly to Moses face to face.[14] God treated Moses like a friend, and Moses wrote down the words God gave him.[15]

The writer of Hebrews reiterates this theme of God's creation by His Word, saying:

> *Through faith we understand that the worlds were framed by the word of God, so that things which are seen were not made of things which do appear.*

Hebrews 11:3

John was the beloved disciple, who walked with Jesus and talked with Jesus and knew Jesus perhaps best of anybody. John tells us:

> *In the beginning was the Word, and the Word was with God, and the Word was God. The same was in the beginning with God. All things were made by him; and without him was not any thing made that was made.*

John 1:1-3

Who is the Word? Jesus Christ.

The Mighty Sun

Now, consider the following verse:

> *The heavens declare the glory of God; and the firmament sheweth his handywork. Day unto day uttereth speech, and night unto night sheweth knowledge. There is no speech nor language, where their voice is not heard. Their line is gone out through all the earth, and their words to the end of the world. In them hath he set a tabernacle for the sun, Which is as a bridegroom coming out of his*

*chamber, and rejoiceth as a strong man to run
a race. His going forth is from the end of the
heaven, and his circuit unto the ends of it:
and there is nothing hid from the heat thereof.*

Psalm 19:1-6

Notice something. It says that the heavens *declare* and the firmament utters *speech* and shows *knowledge*. Every phrase in here is one of information. The title that John gives Jesus is "the Word." There's an intimacy between the declaration of "Let there be light," in Genesis 1 and "the Word" in John 1.

The Psalmist tells us that the heavens declare God's glory. He continues, saying that their measuring line has gone "through all the earth" and their words "to the ends of the world."

The Sun has a role as a bridegroom coming out of his chamber, rejoicing like a strong man running a race. The Sun is running a race? Yes. The Sun is not a thermonuclear bomb going off. It is a light bulb, a very unusual one that's drawing energy from the plasma and converting it to energy we can use on Earth. The Sun has a circuit, and nothing is hidden from its heat.

We discover that the Sun happens to be in a place that makes discovery possible. We can see the corona of the Sun because of its distance from the Earth and its viewable size compared to the Moon. It's this convenient ratio that has allowed us to see the corona during solar eclipses, which has allowed us to develop the study of spectroscopy upon which a large portion of astronomy is based. If the Moon were closer or farther, larger or smaller, or the Sun were visibly larger or smaller, we'd have missed out on the just-so set up that now allows us to see the Sun's corona.

Not only do we have a good vantage point in our solar system to learn about the spectrum of light, we are in an excellent position in our galaxy to research the universe around us. In 2004, Guillermo Gonzalez and Jay W. Richards published a book, *The Privileged Planet: How Our Place in the Cosmos was Designed for Discovery*. They argue that Earth is uniquely positioned for life to flourish, but it's also positioned to feed our curiosity about the wide world – so that we can *discover* the universe around us.

Through the Bible, we are also uniquely positioned to learn about the metacosm. We can study the bigness of the universe – the macrocosm – through the fields of astronomy and astrophysics. We can study the smallest of the small – the microcosm – through the fields of quantum physics. The Word of God also gives us a view into the metacosm, the spiritual world. The present visible world we directly experience is just a digital simulation. The spiritual universe is that which is beyond the simulation, the real universe taking place behind the scenes of our physical eyes.

We find that the Bible is a collection of 66 books written by more than 40 people over a period of nearly 2000 years, yet it's a package that's been deliberately designed to communicate a message from outside the dimensionality of time. It's a message from our Creator to let us know who He is and what He expects of us. Praise God. What can we do to please Him?

> *Through faith we understand that the worlds were framed by the word of God, so that things which are seen were not made of things which do appear.*
>
> Hebrews 11:3

Bibliography

Burnham, Robert Jr., *Celestial Handbook*, Lowell Observatory, 1950-1979, Dover NY, 1978.

Marklund, G.T., *Nature*, 277, 370 (1979).

Peratt, Anthony, *Physics of the Plasma Universe*, Springer-Verlang, 1992, pp.165,166.

Setterfield, Barry, *Anomalies – A Journey of Scientific Discovery* (4 DVDs), www.setterfield.org.

Scott, Donald E., *The Electric Sky*, Mikamar Publishing, Portland, OR, 2006.

Endnotes

1 Norman, T., & Setterfield, B. (1987). *The Atomic Constants, Light, and Time*. Menlo Park, Cal.: SRI International.

2 Barrow, J., & Webb, J. (2006). Inconstant Constants. *Scientific American*, 64-71.

3 Ibid, 65.

4 McKeegan, K et al. (2011). The Oxygen Isotopic Composition of the Sun Inferred from Captured Solar Wind. *Science*, 332(6037): 1528-1532.

5 Staff writers, (2011, June 24). NASA Mission Suggests Sun and Planets Constructed Differently. *Space Daily*. Retrieved on April 25, 2016 from SpaceDaily.com

6 Genesis 11:17-19, 1 Chronicles 1:19.

7 Genesis 19:24.

8 Amos 1:1, Zechariah 14:5.

9 2 Kings 20:8-11, Isaiah 38:7-8.

10 2 Kings 20, Isaiah 38.

11 LIGO. (2016, February 11). Gravitational Waves Detected 100 Years after Einstein's Prediction. LIGO Hanford Observatory News Press Release

12 European Space Agency (2014, April 29). Herschel Discovers Mature Galaxies In The Young Universe. Retrieved May 30, 2014, from http://sci.esa.int/herschel/53992-herschel-discovers-mature-galaxies-in-the-young-universe/

13 For example, Tifft, W. (1977). Discrete States of Redshift and Galaxy Dynamics. III - Abnormal Galaxies and Stars. *The Astrophysical Journal*, 211, 377-391.

14 E.g. Napier, W. & Guthrie, B. (1997). Quantized
    redshifts: a status report. *Journal of Astrophysics and
    Astronomy*,18(4): 455-463.

15 Norman, T., & Setterfield, B. (1987, August). The
    Atomic Constants, Light, and Time. Retrieved January
    2, 2016, from http://www.setterfield.org/report/report.
    html

16 Albrecht, A., & Magueijo, J. (1999). Time Varying
    Speed of Light as a Solution to Cosmological Puzzles.
    Physical Review D, 59(4). Paper No. 043516

17 Overbye, D. (2014, January 8). Halton C. Arp,
    Astronomer, Dies at 86: Sought to Challenge Big Bang
    Theory. *The New York Times*, p. B15.

18 Baggott, J. (September 21, 1991). The Myth of Michael
    Faraday. *New Scientist*, 131:44-45.

19 Burnham, R (1978). *Celestial Handbook*, Lowell
    Observatory.

20 Karachentsev, I., Kashibadze, O. (2006). Masses of the
    Local Group and of the M81 Group Estimated from
    Distortions in the Local Velocity Field. *Astrophysics*,
    49(1): 3–18.

21 Peratt, A. (1989, September). Plasma Cosmology: Part
    II The Universe is a Sea of Electrically Charged Particles.
    World & I, 9, 306-317. Emphases are in the original.

22 Hartnett, J. (2004). *Pleiades and Orion: Bound,
    Unbound, Or ... ?*. TJ, 18(2), 44-48.

23 Gûdel, M. et al. (2008). Million degree plasma
    pervading the extended Orion nebula. *Science*, 319,
    309-312.

24 Marklund, G. (1979) Plasma Convection in Force-
    Free Magnetic Fields as a Mechanism for Chemical
    Separation in Cosmical Plasmas. *Nature*, 277: 370-371.

25 Scott, D. (2006). *The Electric Sky*, Portland, OR: Mikamar Publishing.

26 Davies, P. (2001, November 3). Liquid Space. *New Scientist*, 30-34.

27 Setterfield, B. (2007). Reviewing the Zero Point Energy. *Journal of Vectorial Relativity*, 2(3), 1-28.

28 Dickson, L (2000). Photosynthesis. *Microsoft Encarta Encyclopedia*.

29 Genesis 3:17-19; Romans 8:20-23.

30 Psalm 119:140; Proverbs 30:5.

31 Psalm 138:2.

32 Exodus 33:11; Deuteronomy 34:10.

33 Exodus 24:4; Numbers 33:2; Deuteronomy 31:9.

About the Author

Chuck Missler
President/Founder,
Koinonia House

Chuck Missler was raised in Southern California.

Chuck demonstrated an aptitude for technical interests as a youth. He became a ham radio operator at age nine and started piloting airplanes as a teenager. While still in high school, Chuck built a digital computer in the family garage.

His plans to pursue a doctorate in electrical engineering at Stanford University were interrupted when he received a Congressional appointment to the United States Naval Academy at Annapolis. Graduating with honors, Chuck took his commission in the Air Force. After completing flight training, he met and married Nancy (who later founded The King's High Way ministry). Chuck joined the Missile Program and eventually became Branch Chief of the Department of Guided Missiles.

Chuck made the transition from the military to the private sector when he became a systems engineer with TRW, a large aerospace firm. He then went on to serve as a senior analyst with a non-profit think tank where he conducted projects for the intelligence community and the Department of Defense. During that time, Chuck earned a master's degree in engineering at UCLA, supplementing previous graduate work in applied mathematics, advanced statistics and information sciences.

Recruited into senior management at the Ford Motor Company in Dearborn, Michigan, Chuck established the first international computer network in 1966. He left Ford to start his own company, a computer network firm that was subsequently acquired by Automatic Data Processing (listed on the New York Stock Exchange) to become its Network Services Division.

As Chuck notes, his day of reckoning came in the early '90s when — as the result of a merger — he found himself the chairman and a major shareholder of a small, publicly owned development company known as Phoenix Group International. The firm established an $8 billion joint venture with the Soviet Union to supply personal computers to their 143,000 schools. Due to several unforeseen circumstances, the venture failed. The Misslers lost everything, including their home, automobiles and insurance.

It was during this difficult time that Chuck turned to God and the Bible. As a child he developed an intense interest in the Bible; studying it became a favorite pastime. In the 1970s, while still in the corporate world, Chuck began leading weekly Bible studies at the 30,000 member Calvary Chapel Costa Mesa, in California. He and Nancy established Koinonia House in 1973, an organization devoted to encouraging people to study the Bible.

Chuck had enjoyed a longtime, personal relationship with Hal Lindsey, who upon hearing of Chuck's professional misfortune, convinced him that he could easily succeed as an independent author and speaker. Over the years, Chuck had developed a loyal following. (Through Doug Wetmore, head of the tape ministry of Firefighters for Christ, Chuck learned that over 7 million copies of his taped Bible studies were scattered throughout the world.) Koinonia House then became Chuck's full-time profession.

Beyond Time & Space

- Are there more than four dimensions to physical reality?
- Is it possible to traverse time as well as space?
- Is there a reality beyond our traditional concepts of time and space?

The startling discovery of modern science is that our physical universe is actually finite. Scientists now acknowledge that the universe had a beginning. They call the singularity from which it all began the "Big Bang."

While the detail among the many variants of these theories remain quite controversial, the fact that there was a definite beginning has gained widespread agreement. This is, of course, what the Bible has maintained throughout its 66 books.

Beyond Perception

- Why do scientists now believe we live in a 10-dimensional universe?
- Has physics finally reached the very boundaries of reality?

There seems to be evidence to suggest that our world and everything in it are only ghostly images: projections from a level of reality so beyond our own that the real reality is literally beyond both space and time. The main architect of this astonishing idea is one of the world's most eminent thinkers–physicist David Bohm, a protege of Einstein's. Earlier, he noticed that, in plasmas, particles stopped behaving like individuals and started behaving as if they were part of a larger and inter connected whole. He continued his work in the behavior of oceans of these particles, noting their behaving as if they know what each on the untold trillions of individual particles were doing.

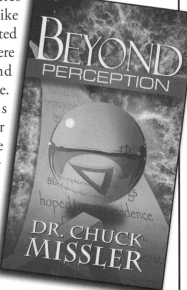

Beyond Coincidence

- Is our universe some kind of cosmic accident, or is it the result of careful and skillful design?
- What do scientists mean by "The Anthropic Principle"?

When compiling the many physical and mathematical subtleties which make up our universe, scientist have discovered that a slight variation in any of them militates against the existence of life. Even at the atomic and sub-atomic level, the slightest variation in any of the primary constants of physics - some as sensitive as one part in over 1,000,000 - cause life to be impossible. Even secular science refers to these appearances of apparent design as the "anthropic principle," since they yield the impression that the universe was designed specifically for man.

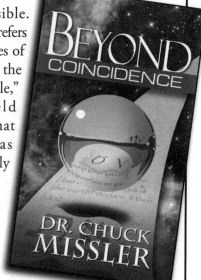

DR. CHUCK MISSLER